Virtue Chic

Virtue Chic

Classy Takes Center Stage

Nikeya Young

November Media Publishing, Chicago IL.
Copyright © Nikeya Young 2017

All rights reserved. No part of this publication may be reproduced, distributed, or transmitted in any form or by any means, including photocopying, recording, or other electronic or mechanical methods, without the prior written permission of the publisher, except in the case of brief quotations embodied in critical reviews and certain other noncommercial uses permitted by copyright law. For permission requests, write to the publisher, addressed "Attention: Permissions Coordinator," at the email address below. November Media
info@novembermediapublishing.com

Ordering Information: Special discounts are available on quantity purchases by corporations, associations, and others. For details, contact the publisher at the email address above.
Printed in the United States of America
ISBN-13: 978-0-9990431-5-8

Cover Design & Interior Design: November Media Publishing
Cover Photographer: Rodney Young Jr. of Young Creative Services
Hair: Ebony Roberts of NK Artistry Salon in Tinley Park, IL
MUA: Per'l Wright, Chicago, IL

DEDICATION

This book is dedicated to my heavenly Father. Apart from God, I would be nothing. Thank you Lord for your unconditional, never-ending love toward me. I live to please you!

To my earthly father, Floyd Green, thank you for your strength, life-lessons, love, and support. No matter how big and "grown" I get, I will always be your "baby girl!" Love you, Daddy!

To my beloved mother, Martha Green, our time together on earth was limited. Yet in just fourteen years you managed to instill enough Word of God, prayers, unconditional love, and wisdom in me to last for years to come! You were the embodiment of virtue, meekness, and strength. As I share some of the same wisdom that you imparted into me, I pray that these seeds of virtue will blossom into a harvest of thousands of dynamic, beautiful, and virtuous women of God! Until we meet again, I love you, and I thank you.

To my precious son, Rodney Price Young III ("R3"): Mommy loves you! This book will be assigned reading for you once you're older so that you will have a written handbook of the type of wife your mother and father are praying for you to marry! To my dear husband Rodney: my mighty man of valor, my King, the love of my life! Thank you for seeing greatness inside of me beyond what I was even able to see in myself. Like the true "producer" you are, you have drawn things out of me and taken them from thoughts, notes in a journal, songs inside of my head, and nurtured them to fruition. It is a privilege and an honor to love, cherish, and be led by such an amazing, Godly, UBER-talented man! The rest of the world is slowly but surely becoming privy to your genius. Oh well. Having it ALL to myself was a privilege while it lasted! LOL! Cheers to many more years of legacy and kingdom building! #TeamYoung

CONTENTS

Foreword by Niki Winston

Introduction

We Are Royals

1

Femininity: A Lost Art

19

No More Toads!
Waiting on God's Prince Charming

35

The Makings of a Virtue Chic Diva

54

Virtue Chic Style & Beauty Files

66

The Virtue Chic Divas Squad

79

Jealousy:
Ain't Nobody Got Time for That!

89

Nice Women Finish First

103

FOREWORD

Church girls have questions, and we want answers! We especially need help in that age in-between: That tricky time between youth-age, where no one really expects a whole lot from us, and that age where we're in the "wisdom" category, expected to be *teaching* the younger ladies. It seems that suddenly so much is expected of us, but we don't know who to look to for the "how." Well, it's our day ladies, because this book has the answers you seek!

This book is the real deal— just like its author. *Virtue Chic: Classy Takes Center Stage* replaces hours of high-quality life coaching on how to be a woman— a REAL woman! Not only is the information contained herein top shelf advisement on the ins and outs of being a godly, virtuous woman, but the author, Nikeya Young, displays the fruit of putting these principles to practice in her own life. Knowing her personally for years, I can tell you that she is a legitimately happy woman, a savvy business woman, a great wife and mother, and has an awesome, solid, godly marriage! Now isn't that what we all want? Why not look for the "how" of being this ideal "Virtue-Chic" woman in someone who's already got it all? I learned so much in reading this book and was encouraged in the things that were already rooted in my heart. I even came to tears several times throughout the book because I was so touched at the love and transparency displayed in Nikeya's stories that came pouring out of her heart.

Whether we just came into the fold or whether we've been saved all our lives, us "church girls"—all colors, creeds, and ages— have similar struggles. Through *Virtue Chic: Classy Takes Center Stage*, we find that we are not alone! Let's go through this together— with the help of Nikeya Young!

-By Niki Winston

INTRODUCTION

If you've picked up this book, chances are, you are a beautiful and virtuous woman of God. You know in your heart that there is nothing wrong with you, but every now and then, it would be nice to hear or see something that provides even the slightest confirmation that being a "good girl" doesn't make you "weird" or "boring." Well Diva, THIS IS IT! *Virtue Chic: Classy Takes Center Stage*, is for every woman who has seen the ratchet reality shows, the over-sexualized women on Instagram, in ads, and in commercials, movies, and music videos galore, and said "I don't see myself in ANY of these women!" This book is for the Godly diva that doesn't feel the need to flaunt her "assets" to fit in with current trends. The woman who is bold and fearless enough to "Stand out," even when she's standing alone. It is also for that woman who has been passed over for "Sister Ratchet" on MORE than one occasion by brothers IN THE CHURCH, causing her to ask herself, "Am I missing something here?" or worse, "Maybe I could learn a thing or two from 'Sister Ratchet' because she ALWAYS has a man, and I'm ALWAYS alone!"

Hang in there, girlfriend! No need to compromise your faith and put yourself on "clearance"! There is nothing wrong with you. There is something very RIGHT with you! It's the rest of the world that has gone insane. We virtuous women have some catching up to do in the PR department. We can't exactly be found on the cover of every magazine or on every television screen. In this day and age, let's face it: we're pretty much UNICORNS! That's why I wrote this book. In fact, *Virtue Chic* is not just a book, it's a MOVEMENT! I'm here to start a #VirtueChic revolution! Join me in bringing class back to the forefront, because let's face it… it's time!

Nikeya Young

We Are Royals

I'm an 80s baby (born in 1981, to be exact). I was only six months old at the time of Princess Diana and Prince Charles's wedding of a century (a fairy tale wedding that was said to have been watched by an estimated global TV audience of around seven hundred fifty million people). Still, I certainly grew to know who Prince Charles and Princess Diana were and their significant roles in history as part of Great Britain's Royal family. Their sons, Prince William and Prince Harry were the subjects of many news reports (despite Princess Diana's desire for the paparazzi to leave her & her children alone so that they could have a normal life)!

As a young child of a single mother battling an incurable illness (Lupus) and living in the projects on the North side of Tulsa, Oklahoma, I would sometimes daydream about what it would be like to be "Princess Nikeya" and live in the royal palace. Surely, it must have been AWESOME to be loved and adored by everyone, be waited on hand and foot, and never experience lack in ANY capacity! Oh, how I longed for that perfect, charmed life! My reality was anything but perfect.

Despite our circumstances, my upbringing was decent. I see that now, but it was difficult to view my mother and I as being blessed and highly favored while we were living in the projects. I was constantly teased at school for not wearing the latest name brands. Martha Green kept me VERY neat and clean at all times, but despite her efforts, I still didn't measure up to what my peers at school thought I should look like. I certainly didn't dress like my cousins (until those rare moments when I was able to score some of their hand-me-downs). Being constantly ridiculed for circumstances that I had no control over, did major damage to my self-esteem during my adolescent years. Not only was I teased about where I lived and that I didn't wear Girbaud, Guess, or Karl Kani (I just dated myself big time, I know!), I was also teased about my looks.

My huge, brown, almond-shaped eyes and naturally full lips have caught the attention of several casting directors who have gone on to book me for various modeling/acting gigs over the past seven years. But back then, my peers didn't appreciate my looks at all! For starters, being dark-skinned wasn't exactly popular back then. All of the boys fawned over the "high-yellow" girls with long hair and hazel eyes. I did not look like this, and so I was ignored (at least until I hit puberty). Then, there was the lips issue. There was a hit sketch comedy show on Fox called *In Living Color*. Jamie Foxx played a character named Wanda. Now Jamie Foxx is an attractive man, but there was nothing attractive about him at all when he came out on stage as Wanda!! He would buck his eyes and toot his lips out as far as he could. I always thought it was hilarious…at first. Then one day on the playground, some kids were talking about an *In Living Color* episode and were doing their best Wanda impression. When I walked by, they all stopped. Then they burst out laughing. "What?" I asked, wanting to be in on the joke. "You look JUST like Wanda!" I was the joke. I never looked at that show in the same way again. I'd watch it and laugh, but when Wanda came out, I'd change the channel!

It took me a while to start seeing myself the way that God sees me instead of through the eyes of others who were obviously dealing with their own hurt and low self-esteem issues (to the point where the only way they felt they could build themselves up was by tearing me and others down). I had to learn to stop wishing that I were someone else (like Princess Diana's adopted black daughter) and learn to appreciate who I was and what I had been blessed with.

Ok, so maybe I didn't live in a middle-class neighborhood or in a two-parent home, but my mother and father loved me dearly, and I was well cared for! Let me tell you, we may have lived in the projects and been on welfare (weekly dialysis treatments made working full-time impossible for my mother), but when Christmas came around, anyone visiting our house would have thought my mother had at least three to five other kids living there! I would have at least twenty boxes of presents underneath the Christmas tree from my parents!

The fact of the matter is, many of the celebrities we often want to trade places with, have very difficult lives! Heck, my beloved Royal family that looked like they had it all together in public lived in turmoil behind closed doors! Princess Diana and Prince Charles divorced in the mid-90s amid affairs and scandal. And even now, the next generation of Royals have had their share of public scandal to deal with as well. Prince William's younger brother Prince Harry, for instance, has made headlines several times for exhibiting behavior that is not fitting for a royal! The definition of **royal** is "of or relating to a king or queen, or other sovereign; descended from or related to a king or line of kings."[1] That's pretty heavy stuff, right? From the time they were born, Princes William and Harry were likely taught what was expected of them as descendants of royalty and heirs to the throne. When you think of royalty, Kings and Queens, Princes and Princesses, Dukes, and Duchesses, you automatically picture people whose manners are impeccable—very stately human beings. When royalty enters the room, everyone around them reacts. Whether with a bow or curtsy or rising to their feet or even moving out of the way,

---

[1] This definition was found at www.dictionary.com.

people respond. It's not just business as usual when you're in the presence of these people. The weight of the authority that they carry is intense, and it's not to be taken lightly. From the moment they were born, William and Harry were not like other children. They were and are royalty. And so are we.

Let's go back to the beginning of mankind. The Book of Genesis explains the nature of who and what we are. After the Lord created lightness, darkness, plants, vegetation, animals, skies, seas, and everything else that makes up this remarkable planet, He created His greatest creation…us. Genesis 1:26-27 in the Amplified Bible says "God said let Us (Father, Son, and Holy Spirit) create man in our own image, after our likeness, and let them have complete authority over the fish of the sea, the birds of the air, the [tame] beasts, and over all of the earth, and over everything that creeps upon the earth. So God created man in His own image, in the image and likeness of God He created him; male and female He created them." WHOA! Do you understand the gravity of what you've just read??! I am sure you've seen this scripture many times in church or in Sunday school, but if you truly understand the magnitude of this scripture, then it should be evident in the way you live your life. Everyone who meets you should be aware that there is something different about you! They may not be able to put their finger on exactly what it is, but there is something unique about you.

The very DNA of the Creator of the Universe is hard-wired into each and every one of us! We are ALL royalty! But here's the thing, we cannot grasp the full benefits of our royalty and all that comes with it unless we have a relationship with God. The way to build a relationship with God is through prayer and studying His word. Doing this helps you to think "God" thoughts, and those thoughts will be followed by actions that will also line up with who and what God has called you to be. Romans 10:17 says, "Faith comes by hearing and hearing by the Word of God." (NKJV). I like this scripture because, simply put, the more you hear something, the more you meditate on it. And the more you meditate on it, the more you believe it! I felt compelled to begin this book by discussing the very nature of who we are because until you grasp your own greatness and your own royalty, you're going to have a tough time processing everything else that I have to tell you. For example, my self-esteem issues during my adolescent years had everything to do with the fact that the voices of my bullies were louder than the voice of God in my mind. My mother tried repeatedly to reassure me, but after hearing negative feedback about myself over and over and over again, I believed it! After graduating middle school and moving on to high school, my young mind finally began the long and tedious process of changing the script. For starters, my mother lost her battle with Lupus just three weeks before my eighth-grade graduation. So here I was in unchartered territory without my best friend in the whole wide world (my mother)!

To say that facing life without my mother was difficult would be a HUGE understatement! But one thing that it did was awaken my survival instincts! After my grief subsided, I was more determined than ever to BE SOMETHING! By the time I graduated high school, I found the courage to enter myself into a beauty pageant. This was a pretty big deal for someone who spent years thinking that they were anything but beautiful. I entered the 1999 Miss Black Tulsa Pageant and competed against women who were in their mid to upper twenties. At eighteen years of age, I took third runner-up. It was the first time I won a trophy for anything in my life! I did many other .out-the-box activities during my senior year that I never had the courage to do before. I entered myself in the state vocal competition and got an "Excellent" rating ("Superior" was the highest rating that you could receive, and Excellent was the second highest). I tried out for the school musical, *West Side Story*, and landed a part as one of the main dancers for the Jets. Slowly but surely, I started to believe in myself more and more. However, I knew that I needed to do something else for this newfound confidence to stick. I needed to spread my wings. Tulsa, Oklahoma wasn't big enough for the dreams and visions that I had in my heart, even back then! It was too…familiar. I remember feeling like I needed a fresh start. I wanted to go someplace where I didn't really know anyone (besides my father, half-sister, and my then boyfriend) so people wouldn't have these pre-conceived notions of what I could do or who I could become.

So, against my aunts', uncles', and cousins' wishes, I applied to and was accepted by DePaul University. I packed my bags and moved to my birthplace, Chicago, Illinois in the summer of 1999. The start of college brought more self-discovery and inevitable growing pains. One thing I can say for myself is that my eighteen-year-old brain had the good sense to know that if I was going to survive the "college jungle," I needed to surround myself with some Christians, and FAST! I began asking around campus to see if DePaul had a Gospel choir. I made up my mind that if they didn't, I was going to start one… somehow. The only explanation that I can give you for this newfound intense desire to make Christian friends almost as soon as I got on campus is that the Holy Spirit put it there. And boy did he know what he was doing! About a month into my first year at DePaul, my high school boyfriend and I parted ways after four years of dating. God was dealing with me so rapidly that he and I just grew apart and had very little in common anymore. For one thing, I back-pedaled on the whole "having-sex-before-marriage" thing and that caused MAJOR problems (more on that later)!

Now bear with me because I know it seems like I've gone way off topic, but I assure you that we are still talking about being "Royals." I promise! I sank into a deep depression after the end of this four-year relationship. I went from one hundred forty-nine to two hundred three pounds by the end of my first year of college. Most people gain weight when they go away for school, but not that much and certainly not that quickly! The good news was that with that last tie to the "old me" severed, God could finally use me for His intents and purposes. Having Godly friends definitely helped me during this period, but more than anything else, I learned to rely on God! I began to study His word and feed on who He said I was. I didn't realize how much of my identity was tied to my relationship until it wasn't there anymore. It was in that moment that I realized that letting other people define me was something that I was no longer willing to do!

There is a biblical story that closely parallels my personal journey. It can be found in the Book of Genesis 12:1-3 (Message Bible): God told Abram, "Leave your country, your family, your father's home for a land that I will show you. I'll make you a great nation and bless you. I'll make you famous; you'll be a blessing. I'll bless those who bless you; those who curse you, I'll curse. All the families of the earth will be blessed through you". That all sounds AMAZING, doesn't it? Then, we peek at verse 4 and see "So Abram left just as God said. And Lot went with him…" (insert DEEP sigh here). God was getting ready to usher Abram, who would eventually become Abraham, into his destiny. God laid out the promise to Abram, and it was AWESOME! However, God specifically said for Abram to leave his family, but we see in verse four that Lot, Abram's nephew, went with him. We do not know the reason that Abram brought Lot along. I am sure he had what he thought were very notable reasons. "I am Lot's mentor, I can lead Lot to Christ…" or "Lot is my favorite nephew and I really feel like he would benefit greatly from the things that God is calling me to do."

Nikeya Young

This sounds thoughtful and nice, but the fact of the matter is that God specifically told Abram NOT to bring any of his family members, except for his wife Sarai, and Abram disobeyed God. God was gracious and merciful to Abram and still fulfilled His promise to him, but that did not cancel out the consequences of Abram's disobedience! The descendants of Abraham and Lot are still at odds to this day!

The biggest lesson to be learned here is that you simply cannot bring everyone along with you! God will almost always instruct you to sacrifice something or leave some familiar things behind to usher you into your greatness! It will be uncomfortable. Some people will think that you are nuts! Do not be afraid when faced with criticism and other forms of opposition! Just focus on the promises of God and let them serve as a reminder to you that it will all be worth it in the end! I am sure that many of us can remember a time in our lives where we made decisions that were contrary to the will of God. However, one thing that we can take away from Father Abraham is to repent, dust ourselves off, and get right back on course with God's plan for our lives!

Virtue Chic "Heart Check":

1.) Is it difficult for you to think of yourself as "royalty"? Why or Why not?

_____
_____
_____
_____
_____
_____
_____
_____

2.) When the devil speaks to you about yourself, what kinds of things does he say?

_____
_____
_____
_____
_____
_____
_____
_____

3.) Now it's time to rewrite the script! Pick five lies that the devil has told you about yourself. Now, for each of those lies, write down the TRUTH about you according to the Word of God. *This is a start, but you may definitely need some more paper for this exercise! When you have more time, do this exercise again on a separate sheet of notebook paper or in your prayer journal.

4.) What "security blankets" have you brought along with you that God meant for you to leave behind as you step into His calling and purpose for your life?

_____

_____

_____

_____

_____

_____

_____

Virtue Chic Confession:

"Lord, you shaped me first inside, then out. You formed me in my mother's womb. I thank you, High God-you're breathtaking! Body and soul, I am marvelously made! I worship in adoration – what a creation! You know me inside and out, you know every bone in my body; You know exactly how I was made, bit by bit, how I was sculpted from nothing into something. Like an open book, you watched me grow from conception to birth. All the stages of my life were spread out before you. The days of my life all prepared before I'd even lived one day. I cannot even begin to comprehend your love for me. From this day forward, I will look in the mirror and admire your work." (Ps. 139:13-16 MSG)

Nikeya Young

Femininity:
A Lost Art

As a former educator, I have witnessed an epidemic of sorts among today's young ladies. With few exceptions, most of the girls that I've seen (at least in urban areas) are... rough. They are loud, they fight at the drop of a dime, and they don't even *smell* like young ladies. And while I wish that I could say I've only witnessed this unladylike behavior among pubescent teenage girls, unfortunately I have seen some full grown adult women exhibiting behavior unfit for a lady as well. There are three main reasons for this unladylike behavior: Parents are not modeling or enforcing femininity for today's youth, society is praising/reinforcing "bad girl" behavior at every turn, and lastly, a lack of fathers has produced many young women who have a mistrust of men and feel that they must "protect themselves." Let's explore each of these a bit, shall we?

Twenty-First Century Parenting

My mother was born in 1948. She didn't become a mother herself until the age of thirty-two. At thirty-two years old, you have pretty much settled into womanhood. Gone are the "finding yourself" days that are synonymous with the teens and twenties. You are older and wiser now. If you were born before the 1960s and 1970's (the decade known best for the "Sexual Revolution" and the height of the Women's Liberation and Civil Rights Movements), you most likely have the unique experience of having been raised by a mother who was a stay-at-home wife and mother who instilled in you the morals and values needed for you to become a good wife and mother someday. You were most likely raised by a mother who was very traditional and wasn't really conditioned to want anything more for herself other than to be a good wife and mother. My mother graduated high school in 1967 and got married in 1968. And I must say, there's a stark difference in the demeanor of the mother I knew and the demeanor of my aunts, who were born after her (my mother was the second oldest of ten children). Now, all children have different personalities, but my latter-born aunts have more feistiness/sass than my mother did! A classic example of this difference could be seen in conversations my mom said she would have with her sisters about how many children they wanted to have when they grew up and left home. My mom would always say she wanted five. My aunts would always tell her she was nuts! As the second oldest, mom had the difficult task of babysitting her lovable, yet behaviorally challenged siblings…a LOT! The others resented having to care for the other kids and vowed to have one child, two at the most when they married and left home. I can remember asking my mom if there was ever anything that she wanted to do or be when she grew up. All she ever wanted was to be a good wife and mother… of five.

I have noticed a trend in mothers who were born after 1960. They became teenagers and graduated high school in the late 1970s and early 1980s. They got married later in life. They went to college (as opposed to heading straight down the aisle after receiving a high school diploma). These mothers gave birth to what is now "Generation Y," better known as The Millennials. These mothers came up in a different time. There were more opportunities available for women, and these women were going to take full advantage of them! They wanted marriage and family too, but they typically possessed a desire to not make the same mistakes as their mothers and grandmothers. They were not going to be dependent on some man for everything! They were going to have something to bring to the table as well. And they were going to raise their daughters to be smart and do the same. The model of femininity that these women presented to their daughters was different than the model that was presented to them. In short, while the Women's Liberation Movement brought us equality in the workplace (to a certain extent, because Lord knows that battle is still going), with each stride we took in order to be seen as equal to men over the years, a piece of our femininity died.

Present-Day Feminism

Nikeya Young

There have been far too many instances throughout the course of history where women have been treated as chattel and have had virtually no agency or control over their own bodies. One of the biggest goals of the feminist movement has been to restore the woman's sense of self. This movement seeks to help women understand that we are not placed on this earth simply for the physical pleasure of men and the birthing of children. We have a purpose! While that school of thought probably has you throwing your bra up in the air and waving it like you just don't care, while simultaneously shouting "YASSSSS," it is important for us to look at the ways in which this whole agency over our bodies concept is lacking balance at best and is unbiblical at worst! No, we are not put on this earth for the sole purpose of being objectified and sexed by men. However, the best way to drive home the point of "I am a powerful and confident woman who is NOT here to be objectified" is NOT to walk around in immodest clothing, wearing cleavage bearing outfits, etc.! We must be careful because the devil often mixes a bit of truth with a lie so that his poisonous agenda is more palatable for us to swallow. Here's what I mean by that: I Corinthians 6:19-20 in the New Living Translation says, "Don't you realize that your body is the temple of the Holy Spirit, who lives in you and was given to you by God? You do not belong to yourself, for God bought you with a high price. So you must honor God with your body." So according to the Word of God, who should really have "agency" over our bodies, God or us? This scripture makes it crystal clear that we are to honor God with our bodies, not use them as tools to manipulate or entice others, or for whatever purpose we see fit!

To get a vivid picture of how today's feminist message blatantly contradicts the Word of God at times, one need only listen to the song "Run the World" by a very popular, African-American, self-proclaimed feminist/singer. The video for this song features an army of women dancing very aggressively and seductively while declaring that they run the world! The fact that the men in the video are decked out in full riot/police state gear is very telling. The message is clear: Men, we are NOT your prisoners anymore! So yes, an analysis of why women are collectively bucking up against the authority of men, whom God designed to provide for and protect us, must address the fact that many men throughout the course of history have either abused their authority" or, to put it frankly, they have been asleep on the job! This lack of covering has resulted in women resenting them and/or feeling the need to "compete" with them, as opposed to respectfully partnering with them as God originally intended. Speaking as an African- American woman, I have found this to be especially true within the African-American community. There is a lot of hurt and pain there, and the devil has used slavery and its crippling aftershocks, to put us (black women) against our men.

We see God's original intention for the partnership of men and women clearly in Genesis 2:18 (AMP) which says, "Now the Lord God said, it is not good (sufficient, satisfactory) that the man should be alone; I will make him a helper (suitable, adopted, complementary) for him". That definitely speaks to a loving, "partnership" between a man and a woman in which both are submitted to one another and ultimately submitted to God. Back to our analysis of the "Run the World" video, the singer is leading her female army against the male-dominated society that has held women back. It is the typical feminist, "Girl Power" message that would have come across just as effectively regardless of who was cast as the male lead. However, the irony of the fact that the leader of the male army that this Black woman and her army are revolting against is a Black male speaks volumes to me. In fact, during the video, black men are repeatedly the recipients of the peaks of her rage. She uses her manipulative feminine powers, or "persuasion," as she calls it, to control two black men into dancing with her team, moving in step with her at her command. Not long after that, she angrily leaps onto the back of another black male placing him in a chokehold and wrestling him to the ground. There are men of several ethnicities in this male army, so she could have chosen any one of them, but they are all black. Whether this was done deliberately or not, I do not know, but I am simply pointing out that it is a clear parallel of one of the biggest problems within the black family structure that we see today: lack of male authority figures in the household (either because fathers are absent, or because as women, we aren't submitting to our men because WE want to be in charge).

Finally, at the very end of the video, her army seductively advances toward the male army. The singer walks up to the leader of the army, again a black man, and literally strips him of his authority (military badge) and slaps it onto her own chest. The man is left with a pained, humiliated expression on his face as all the women proudly salute their "Queen."

Within the African-American community, hundreds of years of slavery has done a number on the very fabric of our family structure. And while we are "free" now in the literal sense, some of the mental chains of the effects of slavery remain. With respect to the loss of our femininity and the "tough" exterior that we "sistas" are automatically known for (whether we like it or not), as soon as we were brought over from our native land, we were ripped from our families. Think about that and what that did to our state of mind. Our men, who were designed by God to honor, protect, and provide for us, were helpless against the cruel slave owners who beat, raped, mistreated, and sold us at will. The message literally beaten into the subconscious of Black women was clear: "We're on our own. Our men are too useless to help us here." The fabric of resentment against our men, perhaps for not trying harder to save us, has been a curse passed down from generation to generation. We have had to be strong and rear children on our own. Our femininity as women was immeasurably compromised, as we HAD to toughen up to survive.

On the black male side, our brothers had to deal with the psychological trauma of being completely emasculated! They had their pride and dignity stripped and beaten out of them. They couldn't protect or provide for their families. They were sold from owner to owner and forced to "breed" with whomever their master wanted them to at the time. So, the curse of being emasculated, baby-making, irresponsible men (with regards to not taking care of their families) was passed down from generation to generation for hundreds of years. There is a LOT of healing that needs to take place within our community for that trust to be rebuilt, for us to be that "helper" of our men that God created us to be…and not their opponent.

So, what now? How do we strike that balance of being ambitious and going after our purpose in life while holding on to our feminine qualities that God has given us? I admit, this balancing act gets to be a little tricky at times, but it is not as difficult as we women often make it out to be. However, we must trust in the Lord! Regardless of our past experiences with men who may have hurt us, failed to provide for us, or protect us, the God that we serve is nothing like man. Numbers 23:19 (NKJV) says "God is not a man that He should lie, nor a son of man, that He should repent. Has He said, and will He not do? Has He spoken, and will he not make it good"?

Femininity in Relationships

This verse is key to remember because oftentimes whenever you get into a discussion of women submitting to their husbands, the knee-jerk reaction from women is something along the lines of "Well what about ME?! He has to do things for me too! I'm not about to be his SLAVE"! Whoa there! God's got your back, Sis! Don't panic! While this isn't a book solely on relationships, I'm going to touch on the issue of submission within a Godly relationship for a second because there are too many women who are saying that they want a Godly man, but they haven't mastered the art of how to treat a man. They are taking their cues from society instead of the Word of God, and the brash, neck-rolling, refusal to submit to their mate as He submits to God is scaring the good brothers off!

So, what is the divine order of how a woman should carry herself in a relationship? If you're not married and you desire to be, you may as well start making it your business to understand the role of a wife from the Father's perspective NOW and save yourself years of unnecessary head-butting and strife in your home later! I Peter 3:1-7 lays it out very plainly. I'm not going to quote it all, but feel free to pause, go read all seven verses, and then come back. I'll wait…

Nikeya Young

To sum it up, God's instructions are: Submit to your husband. In other words, recognize that God has ordained him to be the head of your household. The name of the game is "Follow your man as he follows God." Got it? This is why it's not a good idea to settle for the guy who's "tall, dark, and handsome" but isn't saved! Choose wisely ladies. Ask yourself "Is this someone who is truly being led by God?" If the answer is yes, then this submission thing is way easier because it is highly unlikely that a man who is following the true and living God is going to lead you into a ditch! If you disagree with something he's doing, pray for him. Don't snap off on the man! Verse two says they may be won over "When they observe the pure and modest way in which you conduct yourselves, together with your reverence [for your husband; you are to feel for him all that reverence includes: to respect, defer to, revere him – to honor, esteem, appreciate, prize, and in the human sense, to adore him, that is, to admire, praise, be devoted to, to deeply love and enjoy your husband]."

But God did not leave us hanging! In verse seven, God tells the men that they must be considerate of their wives and know that even though we are the weaker vessel (in the physical sense), we are joint heirs in the grace and favor of God. And get this, ladies…God says that if our men don't treat us right, their prayers will be hindered, or "cut off." That's right! God loves us! He put us under male headship, but not to be "enslaved" or mistreated. If the husband lets this fact slip for any reason, God will check him on it!

Nikeya Young

Virtue Chic "Heart Check"

1.) Think of a time when you have been wounded by a male figure in your life. Pray for the person (or people) and forgive them. Ask God to give you the grace to not view every other man in your life through the lens of your past hurts and experiences.

Study the following scriptures on forgiveness:

"Get rid of all bitterness, rage and anger, brawling and slander, along with every form of malice. Be kind and forgiving to each other, forgiving each other, just as in Christ God has forgiven you." – Ephesians 4:31-32 (AMP).

Matthew 18:21-22 tells us that we must be prepared to forgive over and over again (seventy times seven).

2) What does it mean to be "feminine" in your opinion? Who are some women you admire? Why do you admire them?

Virtue Chic

Nikeya Young

No More Toads! Waiting on God's Prince Charming

Ok, so let's just have this discussion about dating in the twenty-first century, shall we? I already know y'all are going to be skipping ahead in the book for more on this subject matter, especially after that last chapter. So, I may as well give you what you want NOW! I will start off by asking you this very important question: Do you know your God-given purpose for being on this earth? Now you might say "Nikeya, what in the world does that have to do with dating/finding a mate?" EVERYTHING! Here's the thing: God is the ONLY one who can answer that question for you! Oftentimes, we tend to just launch off into our own agendas and expect God to bless it. If you, as a single woman, do not even know your reason for being on this planet, then you will fall into one of the BIGGEST traps that I see women fall into all the time: expecting a man to "complete" you.

Your relationship will become an idol, and we serve a JEALOUS God! Exodus 20:4-5 (NLT) says "You must not make for yourself an idol of any kind or an image of anything in the heavens or on the earth or in the sea. You must not bow down to them or worship them, for I, the Lord your God, am a jealous God who will not tolerate your affection for any other gods." WHOA! God don't play no games! Is there anything wrong with wanting companionship or wanting a husband? Absolutely NOT! However, we must surrender our heart's desires to the Lord and be open to His perfect will and plan for our lives. In short, ladies, we cannot want a man more than we want to love and serve our Father God!

At the start of this book, I mentioned that I became involved in a serious relationship at a very young age. Like most young women who find themselves in this situation, I just KNEW that this was the person that I was going to spend the rest of my life with! And yes, every loving, well-meaning adult in my life told me that getting involved in such a serious relationship while in high school was not a good idea. And like most teenagers, I let the opinions of the naysayers go in one ear and out the other! It would be easy to dismiss my experience back then as a cautionary tale of failed "puppy love," but I cannot tell you how many times I have seen full grown adult women fall into the same trap that I fell into as a teenage girl. We need to see every failure in our lives as a "teachable moment," especially when it comes to failed relationships. If we would be completely honest, every ex in our lives was not this terrible, horrible person. There had to be some admirable qualities about them that attracted you to them in the first place, right? So, when you find yourself at the point of a break up, go ahead and allow yourself to feel the hurt and pain. But PLEASE do not dump that pain all over social media! Seek wise counsel from a spiritual leader at church, or a Godly friend. Journal about the experience and ask yourself, "Ok, what did I learn? What could I have done differently in this situation?" The answers to these two questions should NEVER be Nothing! When you say that there is "nothing" you could have learned, or done differently, you automatically assume the role of "victim." This is a dangerous state to be in because it absolves you of any responsibility in the situation. You cannot grow if you've learned nothing. She who never learns from her mistakes, is bound to repeat them! Even if you dated a guy who was the biggest jerk on planet Earth and treated you like absolute GARBAGE, there are lessons that you can take away from those relationships as well. Yeah, some of these men out here can be slick charmers and fool us, but people will only treat you the way that you allow them to treat you! Never waste a "failure." Always learn something!

From my failed four-year relationship with my high school sweetheart, I learned several key lessons that helped me to grow tremendously during college and throughout my twenties. These very important lessons helped develop me into marriage material and prevented me from stumbling through heartbreak after heartbreak throughout my twenties. Because I didn't hop from relationship to relationship, I was a healed and whole woman by the time God brought my husband into my life. Let's explore some of these lessons:

1) *Know who you are and WHOSE you are!* Now, MOST, if not ALL teenagers have no idea who they are! No one expects them to have everything all figured out at sixteen. Teenagers have so many different voices yelling out suggestions as to who they should be (such as cliques/peers, television, and the music that they are listening to, etc.) The very last thing they need during this time is a full-on, serious relationship. So why are so many teenagers (girls especially) so concerned about finding their "Bae" at an age where they need to be more concerned with preparing for life after high school? Two words: peer pressure! No one wants to be the only single person in their crew of friends at school. No one wants to be without a date to the school dance or prom. It's funny how "peer pressure" can be a major reason that so many single adult women are so obsessed with finding their "Boaz" as well! You see these happy relationships on social media. You have been a bridesmaid in several of your friends' weddings

(perhaps even caught the bouquet), but it appears your turn will never come! You long for companionship. And let's face it, your hormones are racing, and it would be absolutely great to be able to freely have sex as much as you want without the guilt, condemnation, and other consequences that come along with doing it outside of the will of God! Trust me, I am not trivializing any of these concerns or feelings by any means. I am simply saying that there is so much more to you and God's purpose for your life!

The message that I have for my beautiful, single adult sisters in Christ is the same message that I have for my young, Crazy-in-Love, teenaged self: Learn (and fall in love with) who you are. Learn who GOD says you are and what He has called you to do on this earth, and pursue your purpose with pit bull-like tenacity! Literally everything and everyone that you need in your life can be found on the "Yellow Brick Road" of purpose! God's word says it very plainly "And we know that all things work together for the good of those who love God and are called according to his purpose for them." –Romans 8:28 NLT.

There's a lot packed in that verse! If you love God and you are called according to His purpose for your life, ALL things will work together for you…guaranteed! In order to love God, you have to KNOW God, and in order to know God you must spend time in His word and in his presence. Get tuned in to the Father's voice and know it so well that you won't become swayed or distracted by any other voices that would attempt to throw you off track. It really is that simple. We make our lives way harder than they have to be because we want what we want WHEN we want it, but God's timing is always better than ours. Like any good parent, God is not going to give us something that we are simply not ready to receive, and if we go out there and get something on our own (out of season), God is NOT obligated to bless our mess!

2) *Not married? KEEP YOUR LEGS CLOSED!!!* This is a non-negotiable. A "DUH!" for people who call themselves a Christian, if you will. However, MANY believers have struggled (or currently ARE struggling) with the notion that God really does expect you to

abstain from ALL sexual activity until you get married! And just in case some of y'all "deep saints" want to say something to the effect of "Well that was under the Old Testament, or the 'Levitical Law.' Times are different now!" Not so fast! There are PLENTY of scriptures in the New Testament that stress the importance of abstinence/sexual purity. Side Note: It really annoys me when people try to discount the Old Testament as if it has no value! The WHOLE bible is important people! But I digress. In 1 Corinthians the sixth chapter, God says that those who practice sexual immorality (adultery, homosexuality, fornication) will not inherit the Kingdom of God! The Message translation of Hebrews 13:4 says "Honor marriage, and guard the sacredness of sexual intimacy between wife and husband. God draws a fine line against casual and illicit sex." It really does not get any plainer than that!

We know better, but when the going gets tough and our hormones begin to flare up, we try to justify our sin. I TOTALLY did this during my 1st relationship! After all, we were in LOVE! It wasn't like I was out there being with any and everybody! I was only with ONE person, and that person would be my "first and LAST" anyway, so it didn't matter, right? Surely God would "understand." He understands all right. God understands that you "claim" to love Him with "all of your heart" yet you are deliberately disobeying Him for… ***insert guy's name here.*** Is abstaining from sex always easy? NO! Is it absolutely worth it? YES! And I am a living witness that God will keep you if you truly want to be KEPT! With God's help, I was able to abstain from having sex for ten years before I got married. TEN YEARS!!! It is truly possible, and God is faithful and just to forgive you of your sins and cleanse you from all unrighteousness if you confess your sins before Him and ask him to forgive you (I John 1:9 NIV)! Some of the things that I did to help myself stay on track after I repented for my past sexual sins and resolved to remain sexually pure until marriage were: I didn't date much at all (not necessarily because I didn't want to, but guys who were willing to follow God's stance on sexual purity weren't exactly in abundant supply), I surrounded myself with people who would hold me accountable (it's a LOT harder to maintain

Christian standards when you surround yourself with people who are moving in the opposite direction of God!), I read LOTS of books geared toward Christian Singles/Christian Women/Purpose, etc. (you are already on the right track by reading this book), and I found an AWESOME Singles Ministry here in the Chicagoland area entitled "Singles Pleasing the Lord"! They are still around today and going stronger than ever! Please feel free to visit their website at **www.singlespleasingthelord.com**

3) <u>*Be open and honest about what you want in a relationship.*</u> This is another lesson that I took away from my previous relationships. If you express what you want to a man, and that man says something along the lines of "I'd like to get married one day as well, but I'm not really ready for anything serious like that right now." BELIEVE HIM! Perhaps follow up with something like "When do you feel you would be ready for marriage?" Basically, try to get a handle on whether he has some goals that he is working on accomplishing beforehand (like paying off debt or finishing school), or

if he is just a good old-fashioned "Commitment Phobe" type! One of the BIGGEST mistakes that I see women make is trying to "wait it out" until this guy (who has clearly told you he's not ready for marriage) "changes his mind." Or worse yet, many women pretend to be ok with casually dating a man when they truly desire a serious relationship! Don't settle for what you don't want! If you are in a relationship where it's been over six months and you have to ask, "Where is this going?" (and the guy STILL cannot give you a straight answer), leave that dude ALONE! Do not allow some man to keep you "on the hook" and emotionally (and unfortunately for some, "physically") invested in a relationship that is going nowhere! When a man of God is truly serious about you, he will make his intentions known with no gimmicks or tricks!

A True "God" Hook-Up:
My Testimony of How My Husband Found Me

My husband Rodney and I met in college during our undergrad years at DePaul University in the early 2000s.

We briefly dated for about a month during our freshmen year, but we were both on the rebound from previous long-term relationships. I wisely told him that I still needed more time to heal and did not feel that I was ready to enter another relationship so soon. We ended things amicably and remained friends. Since we were both part of the gospel choir at school, we often worked together on music. He was our lead keyboardist, and I was one of the lead soloists. We shared mutual friends and had a genuine respect for one another. He really was a great guy, and I couldn't believe that I was breaking up with him, but God told me to do it because He needed to do some things in me and through me.

Early in my junior year, I moved off campus and spent the rest of my time commuting, and after graduation (in 2003), I didn't really see Rodney again. Fast forward to 2004, I was led by God to attend a new church. On my very first Sunday, I spotted a familiar-looking guy exiting the 9:00 a.m. service. I was heading into the church for the next service. Upon a closer glance, it was Rodney! We greeted each other warmly, and as it turned out, God had just led him to join this church about a year prior to my arrival! He told me that several of our old buddies from the DePaul Gospel Choir attended this church as well. We said our goodbyes, and I didn't really see him anymore for several months. This was a mega church with twenty thousand members and three different Sunday morning services, so that was not anything out of the ordinary. I completed my eleven-week foundation courses, and in the Spring of 2005, I enrolled myself in the ten-week Intercessory Prayer Training class. As I was finishing up my registration paperwork, who did I see? You guessed it: Rodney! We also spotted the mother of another Gospel Choir friend of ours, so the three of us chatted briefly and then found seats in the front row and sat together. We habitually sat together each week for the remainder of the class.

On the last day of class, we were instructed to grab the hands of the person next to us and just pray in the Holy Spirit. Rodney was sitting next to me, so we linked hands and did as instructed. After a while of praying, we were told to be still for a few moments and listen to hear what the Holy Spirit was saying to us. As clear as day, I heard the Spirit say, "You are holding your husband's hand." It startled me! I opened my eyes and looked around because it was almost as if someone else had leaned over and said it to me! At first, I thought, "This is the devil trying to distract me from hearing God!" But over the course of the next year, God gave both of us several confirmations that He was in fact joining us together. Now, even though God had told me that Rodney was my husband, I did not share that information with anyone. The instructions were for me to wait on God's timing and for Rodney to come to me at God's leading.

On a beautiful spring day, March 10, 2006, that moment finally came. Rodney had asked me to join him for ice cream at Baskin Robbins after work. He said that he had something that he needed to discuss with me. I agreed to meet with him, not really knowing what it was about. When I got there, he bought me an ice cream cone and we sat down at a table to chat. I noticed that Rodney appeared to be slightly nervous. He pulled out an apple and gave it to me, and then sheepishly handed me a folded note that read "I REALLY like you! Do you like me? Check yes or no." I laughed hysterically, and of course I said yes! Rodney talked to me about some things that God had been showing him about me and said, "I understand if you need some time to pray about this, but I am not interested in 'casually dating' you. I do not feel that you are the type of woman that one casually dates. I am asking you if you would be willing to enter into courtship with me, and during that courtship we would be preparing for marriage." HELLO! Pretty direct huh? We dated for two years, got engaged on March 10, 2008, and were married in March of 2009! When a man is serious about you, he will let you know! If he is still playing games, it is because he isn't sure that you are the one, and he wants to keep his options open just in case there is something better out there. You deserve better! You deserve a man that values you so much that he seeks God about you, and then approaches you correctly and clearly makes his intentions known. Do not allow anyone to make you think that you are crazy for having high standards. Know your worth. Focus on being a virtuous, purpose-seeking woman of God, and the man that God has for you will come along at the appointed time. Patience is a virtue that we cannot afford to cast aside! God's best is truly better than anything that we can come up with on our own!

Virtue Chic "Heart Check":

This is going to seem like a cruel and unusual exercise to place at the end of a chapter on dating, but the Certified Life Coach in me just CAN'T end this chapter without taking you through this very necessary exercise! I want you to close your eyes and imagine that you are on a beach having quiet time with the Lord. Listen to the ocean waves crashing against the shore. Inhale the ocean breeze. You lead a busy life, so it's refreshing to finally have this peaceful moment free of all distractions. In this environment, you can hear the voice of God clear as a bell! Now, imagine that He has told you that the reason that you have been having such a tough time finding the right man to date is because He wants you ALL to Himself! God has just told you that you are to be a modern-day "Paul" (or "Paulette")! *Open your eyes. What are your HONEST thoughts and feelings at hearing this news? Are you afraid? Angry? Disappointed? If so, why?

_____

_____

_____
_____
_____
_____
_____
_____
_____
_____

My purpose for having you complete this exercise is two-fold:

1. Society often makes women (and men for that matter) feel as if there is something horribly wrong with them if they haven't found their mate by a certain age. Perhaps you have already started to feel the pressure for whatever reason (a high school reunion, relatives asking you if you've met that special someone yet, friends and family trying to set you up on blind dates, etc.). Let's face up to that nagging fear that is lurking at the back

of your mind: "What if I'm single for the rest of my life?"

2. Once you've confronted the possibly of that fear coming to pass, I want you to determine in your heart and mind that you would STILL have a mighty Kingdom purpose to serve on this Earth! It has been my personal experience that the moment I faced up to this fear and had my "though He slay me, yet will I trust Him" moment and decided that I really would be all right if God chose not to honor this request…He honored it! Why? Because I had shown Him that I was mature enough to handle a mate by not desiring a mate more than I desired God's perfect will for my life, whatever it may have been and whether or not it included a man!

The Makings of a "Virtue Chic" Diva

Ok, raise your hand if you've ever read the passage of the "Proverbs 31 Woman" and rolled your eyes. *slowly raises hand*. Trust me, you aren't the only one! This woman seems like an IMPOSSIBLE standard of perfection to live up to! She's a hybrid of Mary Poppins, June Cleaver from *Leave It to Beaver*, Carol Brady from *The Brady Bunch*, and Claire Huxtable from *The Cosby Show* all rolled into one! Again, I won't quote it all, but take a moment to go and read Proverbs 31: 10-31 and then come back. I'll wait…

See what I mean! In addition to being charming and beautiful, this amazing woman in Proverbs 31 also possesses the following qualities, which make her "worth more than diamonds": she is trustworthy (her husband has no reason not to trust her), not spiteful, and domesticated (she can cook, clean, sew, keep a home). She is focused, organized, and wise with money.

Nikeya Young

She is not slothful/lazy, is quick to help anyone in need, and is her husband's pride and joy (others respect him because of his choice in a wife). She always has something worthwhile to say when she speaks, makes sure everyone in her household is productive, and is respected by her children. SHEESH! I know that all of that is a LOT to take in. If only we could all be as virtuous as this Proverbs 31 woman! Well, in this chapter, we will examine the Virtuous Woman and discuss the four main characteristics of being a Virtue Chic Diva.

A Woman on a Mission

This woman is ON IT! She wakes up early every morning full of purpose, drive, and determination! She jumps out of bed, rolls up her sleeves, and is anxious to get started with her day. The Bible goes on to say that she designs clothes (we'll talk more about her style in a bit), is skilled in homemaking, and eager to help anyone in need! She also looks after her family and makes sure that they have what they need. Basically, this sounds like a woman who knows exactly what she was placed on this earth to do. She is a purpose-driven woman. Knowing your purpose simply means that you know why you exist. If you still haven't figured out what exactly your life's mission is, the very BEST way to determine that, is to speak to your manufacturer. Yep, that's right ... GOD.

So, to be clear, there are distinct roles that we play in life: wife, mother, sister, friend, employee, boss, etc., and then there is the task (or tasks) that have been divinely assigned to us by God the father. These tasks are centered around our God-given gifts and talents, and yes, everyone has SOMETHING unique and special that only they can do! You just have to seek God in prayer and read his Word to find it.

There are also practical ways of determining what fields of work best fit your personality (such as the Myers-Briggs test, and other similar personality/career inventory tests). But be careful! These tests give you suggestions as to what might be a good fit for you, but God has the final say, so don't count him out! For example, I've had several tests say that I would make a great schoolteacher. I have a Master of Arts Degree in Special Education and a Bachelor of Arts in Child Psychology, and five plus years of teaching experience in Chicago Public Schools. However, being a schoolteacher is NOT what God wanted me to do, even though I have the gifts of teaching/public speaking! I have been blessed to know my purpose since I was a little girl. All I ever wanted to do was be in the entertainment industry! I wrote songs, memorized EVERY commercial that ever came on television, and loved movies and TV shows as a kid! So how did I end up becoming a schoolteacher? I listened to well-meaning family members who advised me to get a "real job" so that I'd have a solid back-up plan in place and be able to make a decent living. Well, I did that, and I made good money, but I wasn't happy!

If you seek God about your purpose, and He comes back and tells you that you are meant to do something so big that it scares the living daylights out of you because you have NO idea how you're going to pull it off, that doesn't mean you run from your calling! It simply means that you are going to have to trust God to guide you EVERY step of the way! God will give you the grace, favor, and finances necessary to do what He's called you to do. Believe that! I can tell you from experience that I have so much joy and peace every morning now that I am operating in my calling on a full-time basis! God even showed me how to create another income stream to supplement my acting career using something else I love: fitness! I make more teaching Group Fitness classes six to eight hours a week than I would if I worked part-time doing retail twenty hours a week. And it worked out great because I was working out five to six times a week anyway! Now, I just get paid to do so. I'm not saying that you have to do that too, but that's just an example of how God will guide you and show you how to do what He wants you to do!

Another thing that I happily took note of about our "Virtuous Woman" in Proverbs 31 was that her purpose wasn't discontinued once she became a wife and a mother. Oftentimes, women make the mistake of completely abandoning their God-given purpose once they have a family. Yes, things will change somewhat initially, but don't stop doing what God gave you to do!

Your children need to see their mother operating in her purpose so that they can know that the same is possible for them by the grace of God.

Comfortable in Her Femininity

We discussed this in-depth in the last chapter, so I won't spend too much time on it, but it is worth repeating. A "Virtue Chic" Diva is a woman who is proud to be a woman. She has no desire to "compete for headship" in her marriage. She views her spouse as her partner, not as her opponent! She doesn't get offended if a man opens a door for her (yes, I have seen women publicly berate men for this simple act of chivalry)! She is easily identified as a female. Yes, even women who are athletic or who prefer pants over skirts and dresses can still exude femininity and class! The Bible says that this woman's husband has no reason not to trust her. This can be looked at in multiple ways: 1) She's faithful to her husband. 2) Her husband has no reason to ever suspect otherwise because this woman carries herself with dignity and class. To put it plainly, she doesn't use her sexuality to seduce/persuade men into doing what she wants! There is a reason why men will gladly sleep with a woman who puts her goods on display, but would never consider marrying such a woman. If you are constantly displaying your body parts that should only be viewed by your spouse (and your gynecologist), what reason would any potential mate have to ever "trust" that you wouldn't continue to seduce men once you've married him? And furthermore, if you are a woman after God's own heart, you should already know that such behavior grieves the Father, and that alone should be reason enough for you to cover up your goods! Enough said.

Nikeya Young

A Woman of Style

According to Proverbs 31, this woman dresses in "colorful linens and silks," makes her own clothing, and sells her fine garments in the dress shops! Don't buy into the lie that dressing with class/modesty means you must wear burlap sack-looking clothes and walk around looking homely and unattractive. The devil is a LIE! This Virtue Chic Diva is a trendsetter! She has a classy, yet stylish appearance that others want to emulate, so much so that she can turn her style into an entrepreneurial opportunity! She sounds like a woman after my own heart.

Oftentimes we look to the wrong sources for fashion inspiration. Yes, fashion magazines can be helpful, but we must peruse them with a "kingdom-minded" set of eyes. The secular world lives by the mantra, "Sex sells"! Sexual behavior, styles of dress, etc., are used to sell EVERYTHING from yogurt to automobiles. Advertisers are master manipulators. It is their job to appeal to our fleshly desires to elicit their desired response: getting us to buy whatever it is they're selling.

When we go shopping or get dressed in the morning, we tend to subconsciously dress according to our mood, or to the mood that we want to inspire others to feel when they see us. A Virtue Chic Diva has sense enough to know that wearing an outfit that is so tight that it looks like it has been applied with a paintbrush does NOT bring glory to God in ANY type of way! She knows how to dress a way that screams "confident, classy, and fashionable." I have noticed that there seems to be a movement today that says, "Flaunt it if you got it!" And if you aren't flaunting your body, then you need to be more "confident." This could not be further from the truth! True confidence doesn't have to try so hard. The best way that I can explain it is this: Imagine a situation where you had a paper due, but you rushed through it and didn't do your best work. Then, you proceeded to go all out with your title page, and you even put your paper in a nice report cover in hopes that your professor would be so impressed with your outside presentation that he/she wouldn't notice that your content was just ... ok. This is exactly how you come off when you dress in attention-seeking, overtly sexy clothes. It's like you are saying, "Hey, there might not be much depth to me, but ... LOOK AT MY BODY!" Ladies, let's be honest. No one puts on a mini-skirt to impress her other female friends! For all the feminist chitchat about "not needing a man" and whatnot, women certainly do spend a lot of time dressing to impress them! And, that in and of itself is not a bad thing. But as you get dressed in the morning, ask yourself this "What *kind* of man am I attracting with this outfit?" If your desire is to attract a man who loves and honors God, then there is no room for clothes that leave little to nothing to the imagination. I will discuss some practical style tips later in this book to show you some great ways to be virtuous AND chic, so keep reading!

A Woman Madly in Love with God

People who do not fear/revere the Lord frighten me! Without God as your moral compass, you are lost and are subject to do ANYTHING! The Proverbs 31 woman is described as living in the fear of God. Basically, she loves and honors God so much that she doesn't want to do anything that would grieve or disappoint Him. Disrespecting her husband is out of the question, not just because of her love for him, but also because of her love for the Lord of her life who has told her to submit to him! John 14:21 (AMP) says it best: "The person who has my commands and keeps them is the one who [really] loves me; and the one who [really] loves me will be loved by My Father, and I [too] will love him and will show (manifest, reveal) myself to him. [I will let myself be clearly seen by him and make myself real to him]." Translation: God's Word says, "If you love me, then do what I say." Point. Blank. Period. It really is that simple. We make it hard.

Ever the perfect gentleman, the Lord always leaves the choice up to us. He doesn't force anything upon us. We are always free to decide, but we are NOT free from the consequences of our choices.

Nikeya Young

Virtue Chic "Heart Check":

1.) Have you found it especially difficult to submit to the Lord when it comes to your wardrobe? If so, take a moment to ask yourself why. Do you feel that the right man isn't going to notice you unless you "help God out" and "catch the brother's attention"? Pray and ask God to show you how to be stylish and trendy while bringing glory to Him at the same time.

2.) After reading Proverbs 31, what else about the Virtuous Woman do you find difficult to walk out in your own life? Are you unsure of your purpose? Whatever hang-ups you have, write them down, and take them to God in prayer.

_____
_____
_____
_____
_____
_____

Virtue Chic
"Style & Beauty" Files

So, we've talked about the style of the virtuous woman, but I want to delve into this topic a bit more. The truth of the matter is, while there is a LOT of discussion about what NOT to wear as a Christian woman, not much has been said about what TO wear! This mini chapter is dedicated to giving you some great tips on how to be trendy, chic, and HOLY. Yes, all of this is VERY possible! So, let's get to it!

Style Files:

Lay the "Foundation"

Yes, I am talking about wearing the proper undergarments! This is critically important because without laying the proper "foundation," your whole look can be thrown off. Foundational garments include:

bras, girdle/Spanx, underwear, and waist cinchers. Control top pantyhose can also be a lifesaver! I remember working at Victoria's Secret years ago during my senior year at DePaul. One of the first things we did for our customers was to get them fitted for a bra, even if they claimed to already "know their size"! Several studies have been done over the years, and roughly eighty percent of women are wearing the wrong bra size! [2]This can be due to multiple reasons. Our bodies tend to fluctuate, and with each of these fluctuations, our band (the part that wraps around the back) or cup size can change at any phase in our lives. Bottom line, don't assume that you wear the same bra size that you wore last year (or even six months ago)! Get fitted. Your shirts and blouses will hang so much better on you…TRUST ME!

---

[2]For more information, visit womenshealthconversations.com/womens-health/women-still-wearing-wrong-size-bra. This statistic has been tossed around for many years, often by lingerie specialists in department stores who have done their own studies by conducting free bra fittings in their stores and finding that on average, 8 out of 10 of their customers are wearing the wrong size bra.

In terms of underwear, the key here is knowing which pair of undies to wear underneath your clothes. And let's just dispel one myth RIGHT NOW: Christian ladies CAN and should wear thong underwear! Ladies, stop making that face. I know many of you have probably thought or have been told that only "naughty girls" wear thongs, but nothing could be further from the truth! I love you too much to let you think that you are being "more holy" as you walk around with visible panty lines! There is nothing cute about VPLs! If you're wearing a thong with a skirt (to prevent VPLs), you can, and should also pull on a girdle over that to prevent any "Marilyn Monroe" moments. There, problem solved!

Spanx and pantyhose are lifesavers in terms of "smoothing you out" underneath your clothes. No lumps, bumps, or cellulite! Again, not a good look! Yes, I said wear thongs (VPLs are the WHOLE DEVIL), but wear shapers or control top pantyhose over them when needed for extra support. Spanx come in various lengths to accommodate whichever bottoms you choose to wear (pants, skirts, shorts, dresses, ball gowns), so grab a few! And you may as well invest in a good sturdy pair of Spanx because the cheap imitations will literally "leave you hanging" when you need them the most!

Dressing for Your Body Type

Now that we've discussed the proper undergarments, let's discuss the different body types and what looks best flatter each shape. Here we go…

Round: You carry most of your weight in your midsection & generally have a fuller, rounder torso.

If this is you, you want to try and create the illusion of a long torso. Wear a good supporting bra that lifts and supports the "girls," and a V-neck top— make sure that "v" doesn't plunge too low! —and a wide belt around the waistline to create a waistline. Slim-fitting boot cut jeans work great. Knee-length skirts that show just the right amount of leg paired with a decent sized high heel works great too (again creating a lengthening illusion).

The Triangle: Smaller up top and fuller on the bottom (also known as the "Pear" shape).

You want to avoid blousy, over-sized sweaters that tend to add more weight on top. Dark-washed, wide leg pants will create a slimming effect in the thigh area and make you look long and lean. Boatneck tops work well for this body type as they broaden the shoulders, which in turn balances out wider hips. Also, an A-line skirt is your BEST friend! Steer clear of pencil skirts if you already have wider hips. Pencil skirts will make your hips appear even larger.

The Inverted Triangle: Heavier on top & slimmer on the bottom.

Wearing darker colored blazers or tops is a neat trick for minimizing the bust area. You can wear V-necks and scoop neck shirts (remember to make sure that the cut isn't too low). Again, you can also play up your smaller waistline by wearing belts, wrap dresses, etc. A-line dresses and skirts look GREAT on this body type as well because they create the illusion of a fuller lower body. Wide leg pants, such as gauchos, are ideal. You want to steer clear of tapered-fit bottoms.

The Hourglass: The shape that everyone wants! Full bust, small waistline, full hips.

Nikeya Young

I happen to be an hourglass, and this shape, while highly desirable, poses one problem: this shape is naturally sexy/appealing to men with little to no effort needed! So yes, dressing modest while possessing an hourglass shape is more difficult, but not impossible. One thing I can tell you is, DON'T wear over-sized cardigans, boxy/overwhelming tops, baby-doll dresses, etc.! Unfortunately, that's the first thing that most church folks want to do to people who have this body type because it is viewed as a PROBLEM! Their mantra is to COVER IT UP with as much fabric as humanly possible!

While we don't want to flaunt ourselves too much, we also don't want to add twenty-five pounds to our body by wearing clothes five sizes too big either! Here are some looks for you to try:

- High-waisted jeans to accentuate the waist, paired with a long blouse and a wide belt.

- Wrap dresses with a cami underneath, or V-Neck tops and dresses that don't plunge lower than three fingers below the collarbone.

- Pencil skirts that extend slightly below the knee.

- A-line dresses and skirts.

The Rectangle: "Boyish" Figure

For this body type, you want to cinch your waist with wide belts or wear dresses and tops with ruching on the sides to create the illusion of an hourglass shape. Boot cut pants look great on this body type! Other style must-haves for you are a fitted blazer, and fit-and-flare skirts. Accenting the waist area helps to add dimension to your body.

"Inside Out" Beauty Files

Now that you have some tips on how to dress for your body type, let's discuss some basic beauty tips to help you look and feel your best!

1.) What's your skin regimen? - I was blessed to have inherited awesome skin genes from my mother's side of the family. That being said, I don't take this for granted! EVERY woman should have a daily skin care regimen. The products that you use will vary depending on your skin type (dry, oily, normal, or combination), but the basics that every woman needs are: a cleanser (preferably one that is a gentle "no soap" wash that won't dry out your skin), a toner (I use either Sea Breeze or Witch Hazel for this step, but again, I'm a little "old school." These products have been tried-and-true for me, but some may find Sea Breeze to be too harsh for their skin). You also need a moisturizer (lightweight, oil-free with an SPF of 15 or higher – EVEN if you are African-American! Our melanin does not exclude us from sun damage), and a face mask treatment once or twice a week to prevent blackheads, blemishes, or breakouts. I have normal-to-oily skin. My t-zone (forehead and nose area) tends to get oily while the rest of my face is dry. For my cleanser, I use Noxzema. I have been using Noxzema since I was around eight years old, and I swear by it! Then, I go over my face with the Toner/Sea Breeze to remove excess dirt/oils. For a moisturizer, I usually just dab a quarter-sized amount of Lubriderm all over my face and massage it in, and I'm out the door! However, I recently discovered this awesome tinted moisturizing cream/makeup by Maybelline called "Beauty Balm" (BB for short), and I love it! It's great for those days when you kind of want to wear some makeup, but not really, and it has been a lifesaver for me during the summer months! There are eight benefits of Beauty Balm. It blurs imperfections, brightens, evens skin tone, smooths, hydrates, enhances, protects with SPF 30, and has zero oils and heavy ingredients. Be sure to wash your face at least twice a day (in the morning and again before bedtime), and DEFINITELY after a workout!

2.) Drink water! – It's amazing how many people readily admit that they don't drink water or have maybe 2 cups of it per day. Our bodies are made up of about sixty percent water. So, if you are not drinking at least eight cups of water per day (sixty-four ounces), then chances are, you are dehydrated! If you want to give your water some flavor, try putting fresh lemon, mint leaves, and cucumber slices into your water. This not only tastes great, but also detoxes your system. So be prepared to go to the bathroom more frequently! The results are worth it.

3.) EXERCISE! - There are many amazing benefits to daily exercise. According to the Aerobics and Fitness Association of America (AFAA), here are eight essential benefits that you get from doing just thirty minutes of cardio (biking, walking, running, swimming, etc.) per day: lower risk of early death, heart disease, stroke, high blood pressure, adverse lipid blood profile, type 2 diabetes, metabolic syndrome, colon/breast cancer (and ALL of that is just benefit #1!), prevention of weight gain, weight loss, improved cardio/muscle fitness, prevention of falls, improved cognitive function, better health, reduced obesity, and prevention of depression. There are more benefits, but these alone are DEFINITELY worth getting up and heading to the gym! Can't afford a gym membership? No worries. Go to the park and do a brisk walk around it for thirty minutes. Bad weather? Look up a woman named Leslie Sansone and purchase her "Walk Away the Pounds" DVD's! No, she did not pay me to endorse her products in my book. I found out about her at-home workouts from my mother-in-law and my husband and I LOVE them! This woman is fifty-five, and she looks amazing! The workouts are very easy to do. You literally walk back and forth in your living room to the tempo of the music. Each mile is timed (between 13-15 minutes per mile), and when you have reached the end of the mile, she will say "Congratulations! You just did a mile!" The cost of the DVD is around $10 at Wal-Mart. And there you have it! I have literally taken away ALL your excuses, so get moving and take care of your temple!

Nikeya Young

Virtue Chic "Heart Check":

1.) Be honest with yourself. Are you taking the best possible care of your temple? If not, what are some of the largest obstacles that stand in your way? Write them down and then pray and ask God to help you to develop discipline in the area of healthy diet and exercise.

_____

_____

_____

_____

_____

_____

_____

2.) Are there any items in your wardrobe that could be a potential "stumbling block" to any man who is in your presence while wearing these items? For example, do you have any dresses that are too short or too tight, cleavage-bearing tops, miniskirts, etc.? Does the thought of getting rid of these items anger or sadden you in any way? Why? Talk to God about your feelings on surrendering your wardrobe to him. Be willing to seek to please him above ANY and everyone else!

Nikeya Young

The Virtue Chic Diva's Squad

They say if you really want to learn more about the true character of a person, look at their closest friends. No one understands this better than a Virtue Chic Diva! This woman and her friends are seriously #SquadGoals! Here are the kinds of friends you absolutely MUST keep company with as a stylish, anointed, and Virtue Chic Diva!

The Intercessor – This woman can pray down fire from heaven! If the devil is ever stupid enough to try and run up on you, this is the friend that you can call (no matter what time of day or night) to pray you through any and EVERY situation! Granted, all your friends have some sort of prayer life, but THIS ONE has Jesus on speed dial!

Why she's important: An intercessor is willing to stand in the gap for those in need. This person has integrity to spare, which is why they can get a prayer straight through to the throne room! They are also objective, and they have genuine empathy in their hearts for people in general. A lot of times, they will sense that you need prayer before you can even bring up the issue to them.

Having an intercessor on your team is key because, let's face it, YOU are usually the person that all your friends run to for prayer and advice. And while that's not necessarily a bad thing (it means you're trustworthy), it definitely helps to have someone that you can run to when you need prayer as well!

The Overachiever: If you are the smartest person in your circle, then you need to broaden your circle! After all, iron sharpens iron! Every diva needs to have a friend that inspires them to do better, reach higher, and think BIGGER! The "overachiever" is that friend. She isn't arrogant with flaunting her accomplishments in your face to play the "One-up" game. On the contrary, she just makes stuff happen! She will bring some things up in conversation, but she's not one to broadcast her every move. She just gets stuff done! When you speak to her on the phone, you have conversations about a cool business and branding podcast she caught this morning on the way to work, or the latest New York Times Best-Sellers list. She sends you invites to the coolest conferences, empowerment events, and such. Bottom line, she's a BOSS Chick who is going places, and this doesn't intimidate you one single bit…because so are you! Together you two will make huge kingdom impact!

The "Day One" Friend: You've known each other for longer than ten years. Maybe even since grammar school! You can finish each other's sentences. She refers to your parents as Mom and Dad, and makes a beeline for your fridge whenever she comes by to visit. Calling this person a "friend" almost seems sacrilegious because she's WAY beyond that! She's family. Friends like these are rare in this day and time. As we grow and mature or relocate, we tend to lose touch with friends from our past. Depending on what our past was like, many times it's best to cut all ties with who we once were as we walk in the newness of who we are in Christ. But if you've managed to hold on to a friend like this one, you've got a jewel!

The Accountability Partner: No one needs to be surrounded by a bunch of "Yes Men"! This friend is special because she keeps you in line whether you like it or not. She is not afraid to risk you being ticked off at her for a bit when she tells you what you NEED to hear, but didn't quite WANT to hear! She isn't disrespectful or condescending about it either. She speaks the truth in love. In fact, she usually starts off by saying, "You know you're my girl and I love you, but (*insert words of wisdom and accountability here*)". She is the friend that says "Donuts for breakfast? I thought you said you were trying to lose weight? Let's ditch that donut. I'll buy you a green smoothie instead." Or, she may just wrestle that donut out of your hand and say "NOPE! I am doing this for your own good! You told me to help you if you fall off, and that's what I'm doing!" And in that moment, you won't know whether to hug her or punch her in the face—*don't punch her in the face*! She REALLY does love you. She will tell you to delete your ex's number and remove him from all your social media platforms because he's no good for you and she's tired of seeing you settle for being placed on this dude's "standby" list when he clearly has zero intentions of getting his act together! She keeps you humble.

She is valuable because she keeps it ALL THE WAY REAL with you! She is also a great listener and can take a secret to the grave. This kind of friend is crucial to your growth and success! There may be seasons when you resent her words of wisdom and accountability, but do NOT shut her out! God has placed her in your life for a REASON. Think of her as the Holy Spirit in human form. This kind of friend will never steer you wrong!

The "Fun" Friend: All work and no play makes for a very dull and miserable life! This friend makes sure that you get out and have some much-needed FUN! She is the first person you call if there's a cool concert coming to town or a chick flick in theaters that you already know your boyfriend or hubby ain't about to go to with you! She is the funny one in the group that makes you laugh to the point of tears. She's your shopping buddy. If you have kids, she's one of the first people you ask to babysit because your kids always have just as much fun with her as you do! You and this woman are pretty much "Lucy and Ethel 2.0" when you get together. You need people like her in your life because life comes at you fast and hard at times. The Bible says in Proverbs 17:22 that "A cheerful heart is good medicine, but a broken spirit saps a person's strength" (NLT). Medicine is a great word to describe this dear friend! She manages to cheer you up even when cheerful is the LAST thing you want to be!

3 Types of Friends to Avoid

The Gossip: This "friend" is always telling you the "tea" on everybody around you, so much so that you are VERY careful about the information that you share with her! Basically, if you wouldn't post it on a billboard, you don't share it with this person! This person is also coming back and telling you what other people are saying about you. Ever wonder why people feel so comfortable saying bad things about you in front of this "friend"? A friend that you cannot trust isn't really a friend at all. And at this stage in your life, you are too grown to play "high school"!

The Promiscuous Friend: This friend changes up guys like she changes her shoes! She may or may not dress provocatively as well. Perhaps men have hurt her in the past, so her attitude is "get them before they get me"! But you've seen her mistreat perfectly good men as well. She is not the type to settle down at all. This is the type of person that you want to keep on your prayer list, but NOT someone that you want to have in your squad as one of your main friends!

The Frenemy: "You can't be friends with someone who wants your life." – Oprah Winfrey

The Frenemy is usually someone that you've let stay in your life way past their expiration date due to some sense of obligation: you've known them since high school, you're related to them, or they helped you out in a pinch. Whatever the reason, you know in your heart that this person is not a true friend. You two have a falling out at least once a month, and you swear that you're through with them for good … until they come back crying and begging you for forgiveness and telling you that you are their only true friend. You forgive them, and then before you know it, they have hurt you again! The Frenemy's biggest problems are jealousy and envy. When you are going through a rough time (a break up, job loss, financial struggles, etc.), they will share words of comfort and be your shoulder to cry on. But as soon as you are prospering, their attitude toward you shifts, and they suddenly do not have time to be bothered with you. Despite the times that you were there to support them for life events and successes, when it's your turn, they are nowhere to be found! They do not necessarily care if you are doing well, but will resent you with a quickness once you start doing better than them! If you mention a guy that you think is cute, the next thing you know they are dating that guy. They are the queens of the "One-Up" game! As soon as you mention a recent victory in your life, they quickly come up with something to top your news (even if they have to flat out lie and make something up)! They may care about you on some level, but their own hurt and insecurities will not allow them to truly be happy for you (or anyone for that matter). Your success threatens them. If there is anything in their power that they can do to stunt your growth, they will do it! This is the friend who is quick to tell you to leave your boyfriend or husband after every little argument. Maybe they want your guy for themselves? Perhaps they just want you to be single because they haven't met that special guy just yet. Bottom line, this friend is BAD NEWS! Let them go, and do not allow them to try and make you feel guilty for no longer befriending them!

"Do not be deceived: Bad company corrupts good morals." – I Corinthians 15:33

Virtue Chic "Heart Check":

Take a few moments to think about your circle. Are there some friends in your life that you've let linger past their expiration date? Do you have people in your life who motivate you to be all that God has called you to be? Spend some time in prayer and ask the Holy Spirit to reveal to you anyone who does not serve you best in this season. Also ask Him to reveal people who DO serve you best in this season. Ask Him to show you mentors, accountability partners, friends, etc. who may be right under your nose. Write down what He tells you.

_____

_____

_____

_____

_____

Nikeya Young

Jealousy: Ain't Nobody Got Time for That!

If you, or someone you know has ever said, "Most of my friends are guys because women are too jealous and catty," then buckle up! We are about to dive into the topic of jealousy and envy. First of all, it is important to note that jealousy and envy issues are not exclusive to women! Men struggle with this issue too, but men tend to be less vocal about their feelings than women, and so their feelings of jealousy are expressed differently. We will begin by defining these two terms. Though they are used interchangeably, jealousy and envy are not the same thing. Richard Smith, Ph.D. explains the difference between the two perfectly: **Jealousy** occurs when something we already possess (usually a special relationship) is threatened by a third person. **Envy** occurs when we lack a desired attribute enjoyed by another.[3]

I often say that social media is a blessing and a curse for many reasons, but one of the main reasons is because seeing the lives of everyone in your timeline can often lead to feelings of envy if you are not careful! For example, let's say you are single, and you aren't particularly feeling bad about it today. You're happily going about your business, earning your degree and pursuing your dreams. Then, you log onto Facebook or Instagram and it seems like everyone in your news feed is blissfully happy in their marriages or dating relationships. Suddenly, envy sets in, "Why can't I have that?" you ask yourself. The relationship issue is just one example! Too much social media can cause you to envy just about every aspect of your friends' lives! The vacations they take, their cars, their budding careers, you name it! Before you know it, you have gone from

---

[3] "What is the Difference Between Envy and Jealousy?" Joy and Pain. Richard Smith Ph.D, January 3, 2014. Web. PsychologyToday.com .

being in a happy place with where you are in life, to not being satisfied with ANY aspect of your life!

There is absolutely NO PLACE for either one of these toxic emotions in the lives of any Christian! When jealousy or envy raises its ugly head, we must not let it fester, or it can have disastrous results! Let's look at a few biblical examples of jealousy and envy to explore this even further.

Cain Envies Abel (Genesis 4:4-8, AMP)

In this passage of scripture, Cain (a tiller of the ground) and his brother Abel (a keeper of the sheep) each made a sacrifice (offering) unto the Lord. Abel offered the fat portion of the firstborn of his flock. In other words, Abel offered unto God his "best." Cain gave God an offering too, but it was not his "best" sacrificial seed, and the Lord did not regard Cain's offering with the same respect that he did Abel's offering. Cain was FURIOUS! I can imagine he said something like "God always favors Abel over me! It's not fair!" And God didn't just leave Cain to stew in his anger. He said to Cain, "Why are you angry? And why you do look sad and depressed and dejected? If you do well, will you not be accepted? And if you do not do well, sin crouches at your door. Its desire is for you, but you must master it." God clearly warned Cain about the dangers of his envy and anger leading to sin, but Cain did not heed God's warning. Instead, he lured his brother Abel into a field and killed him.

There will be people in your life who will be jealous of the blessings that God is heaping upon you, but like Cain, they don't want to put in the "work" that is necessary to get what you've gotten! The fasting and prayer, the sacrificial giving, crying out to God in praise and worship, making mistakes and learning from them, seeking and heeding wise counsel … no one sees any of that. And when they ask you how you got "such and such" and you tell them, oftentimes they won't heed your advice and will choose to just "hate" on you instead. It is very annoying, but you must keep them lifted up in prayer, because, like Cain, sin is crouched at the door! If they don't check their emotions of envy toward you and anyone else they might be envious of, the results could be disastrous!

Rachel and Leah (Genesis 29 and 30)

I have a half-sister, but I did not grow up in the same house with her. I grew up around cousins who were like sisters to me. Nevertheless, I can attest to the fact that whether it's sisters or cousins, sibling rivalry is real! It is a part of life, and it can only grow as deep-seeded as you allow it to grow. As you grow older, most people can bury the hatchet, but then there are some who carry their feeling of bitterness, jealousy, and envy toward their sibling well into adulthood.

Such was the case with Rachel and Leah (over a MAN of all things)! In Genesis 29, we see that Jacob (later named Israel) fell in love with Rachel, the youngest daughter of Laban, from the moment he saw her. The Bible describes her as very beautiful and attractive. When Jacob saw his uncle, Laban, he told him that he was in love with his daughter, Rachel. Not wanting to have his nephew working for him for free,

Laban asked Jacob what would his wages be? Well, it was a no-brainer for Jacob! He wanted Rachel! Well, you know the story. Jacob (a trickster himself) had met his match! After working for seven years to receive Rachel as his bride, per he and Laban's agreement, Laban snuck his older, less attractive daughter Leah into the tent with Jacob! Needless to say, Jacob was not happy when he woke up the next morning and saw his new "wife" Leah in the bed! After hearing Laban's poor excuse (lie) about it not being custom to marry off the younger daughter before the older one, Jacob finished his marital week with Leah, and after that, he was given Rachel, the woman he TRULY loved in the first place.

I am not sure what Rachel and Leah's sisterly relationship was like before Brother Jacob strutted into town, but this hot mess of a marital agreement certainly did not help! In Genesis Chapter 30, we get to see just how the epic rivalry played out. Let's just say that Jacob had his hands FULL! As I mentioned earlier, *envy* occurs when one lacks a certain attribute of another. *Jealousy* occurs when one is worried that another person will take something that is theirs. Well, Rachel and Leah were both jealous AND envious of one another! Can you imagine what it must have been like to be Leah? To watch everyone "ooh and ahh" over how beautiful your little sister is and totally ignore you as if you were the help? To even be in the position to where you (and your father) felt that the ONLY way to ensure that a man would EVER marry you is to "trick" him into doing so? Ouch! Talk about a blow to the ego!

Rachel, on the other hand, suffered from what I like to call "Pretty Girl Privilege." When you are the type of woman that is so FINE that a total stranger sees you out shepherding a flock of musty sheep and falls SO head-over-hills in love with you that he voluntarily indentures himself to your father for SEVEN YEARS just to get with you, you may or may not let that kind of attention go to your head! Rachel was probably used to being favored because of her extraordinary beauty. I'm sure that it didn't sit too well with her when she learned that she would be "sharing" her husband with her sister Leah. Luckily, Rachel knew that her man didn't want Leah and that SHE was the only reason that Jacob would touch Leah with a ten-foot pole. So, Rachel let

Leah have her moment (wedding feast week), but she figured after that, things would be back to "normal" and she'd have Jacob's love and affection all to herself once again. What Rachel did not foresee was the fact that she would have a reason to be jealous and envious of her sister! But lo and behold, God saw that Leah was despised by her husband and opened Leah's womb. Leah bore Jacob four sons (Reuben, Simeon, Levi, and Judah). Meanwhile, Rachel was barren! My how the tables had turned! All of a sudden, Leah was able to do something for Jacob that Rachel could not do, and Rachel did not like that ONE bit! I imagine that Leah, thrilled to FINALLY be able to "one-up" her sister in something, totally rubbed her children in Rachel's face.

Not one to take things lying down, Rachel became desperate to have children! In fact, she was so desperate that she gave her maid Bilhah to Jacob so that he could bare children for Rachel through the maid! Finally, Rachel had children of her own (sort of)! Now Leah was worried. Having children was the only way to get Jacob to show her any kind of attention. Leah knew Jacob did not love her, but at least he was proud of the sons that she had given him to pass down his legacy. That made her walk a little taller, and I'm sure that she and Jacob had more interaction with one another as they tended to the needs of the children. But now that Rachel had a child too, Leah felt threatened! Rachel had "a" child (through a maid!). Leah had FOUR biological sons. She ceased bearing children for a time after that, but the fact remains that Leah, with her four sons, felt jealous of Rachel because of her surrogate son (Dan). Soon, Rachel's maid had another son (Naphtali), and that was the straw that broke the camel's back! Rachel was catching up! Leah had to act fast!

Are you all starting to see a pattern here? Nothing about jealousy and envy is rational. When you yield yourself to jealousy, you yield yourself to a lifestyle of CONSTANTLY jumping through hoops in hopes of outdoing or "one-upping" someone. You get so caught up that you cannot even appreciate the blessings that God has already given you. Nothing is ever enough! Leah could no longer appreciate the blessing of being given four beautiful children who loved her unconditionally, though her husband did not. Rachel was married to a man who toiled SEVEN years for her. She was gorgeous, and she knew it. She was privileged and favored over her less-than-attractive sister in every way, so why was it so difficult for Rachel to let Leah enjoy this one win? This insane "Child birthing Olympics" continued on with Leah giving her maid Zilpah to Jacob as a secondary wife. Zilpah bore Jacob two sons. Then Leah's womb opened once again, and she gave birth to two more sons AND a daughter! Rachel finally got her wish and gave birth for the first time, to a son whom she named Joseph. She eventually gave birth to a second son, Benjamin, but she died shortly after giving birth.

Overcoming Jealousy and Envy

If you are suffering from being jealous or envious of someone, please take the time to purge these two ugly emotions from your life IMMEDIATELY, because they never produce good fruit! Here are some crucial steps to overcoming jealousy and envy:

1.) <u>Identify your triggers</u>. Be honest with yourself! I am all about keeping a journal because you can be as frank and upfront with yourself without having to worry about anybody judging you. So, if you find yourself rolling your eyes whenever you come across a friend's happy relationship post on social media, take a moment to think about why that post bothers you so much (as opposed to subconsciously or consciously attacking the person/people who posted it). For example, you see that a friend has posted something along the lines of "My husband made me breakfast in bed and bought me roses this morning! #BestHusbandEver." You roll your eyes and say something to the effect of "So what? Who cares?! UGH! She's always trying to front like they have this perfect marriage. I'll bet they are just MISERABLE behind closed doors!" Perhaps you even post a "subtweet" (subliminal attack in which you are calling out a person's behavior without saying any names) and say something to the effect of, "If you were really happy in your relationship, you wouldn't feel the need to broadcast it all over social media. Who are you trying to convince? Us or yourself?" There! That should fix Little Miss Perfect, right?

Of course, this is a silly example, but we've all seen this before, and if we're honest, we may have even done something like this before. If so, no condemnation! Let's just get to the root of the matter. You could be absolutely right. What if "Little Miss Perfect" really doesn't have a perfect marriage and she is going through all the trouble of posting daily statuses like she has it all together, but she is miserable behind closed doors? Even if that's true, shouldn't your response be to PRAY for her instead of relishing in her misery? You could also be completely wrong, and Little Miss Perfect really could have a marriage made in heaven! The fact of the matter is, several other people in your timeline saw the same post that you saw. However, instead of getting envious, they hit the "like" button and left comments about how much it blessed them to see a Kingdom marriage.

Whether you were right or wrong in your assumptions, you need to ask yourself, "Why did that bother me so much?" If you're honest, you were most likely bothered by that status because you are frustrated with being single. Or perhaps you are married, but your marriage doesn't look anything like Little Miss Perfect's marriage, and you REALLY wish it did! Loneliness, a lack of satisfaction with your career, or life in general, can leave you with feelings of insecurity or inadequacy. When those feelings are not processed and prayerfully submitted to God, they give way to jealousy and envy, and as we have observed through the biblical examples, there is NOTHING rational about jealousy and envy! These two emotions can turn you into a mean, cynical, and hypercritical person!

2.) Trust in the Lord! On the surface, it may seem like trusting in God has nothing to do with your feelings of jealousy and envy, but I beg to differ! Once you have a divine revelation of how much God loves you and the fact that we serve the God of "more than enough," then you will realize that you really have no reason to ever be jealous of anybody! There is no scarcity in God. If someone you know married that fine brother in church that you have had your eye on, so what?! He is not the last godly man on Earth. And he was clearly not your husband, or God would not have given him to someone else! Someone else got a new house? Good for them! Romans 12:15 tells us to rejoice with those who rejoice! When you can do that, the windows of heaven will open over your own life as well. Acts 10:34 tells us that God is no respecter of persons, meaning God does not play "favorites"! We are all God's children and He loves all of us the same. I keep hearing God's words to Cain in Genesis 4:6-7 (AMP) before Cain allowed his envy to consume him and cause him to murder his own brother: "Why are you angry? And why you do look sad and depressed and dejected? If you do well, will you not be accepted?" Trust that God is not out to withhold anything from you. Walk uprightly. Tithe! Make sure that you are doing your part, and God will always do his!

<u>3.) Fast from social media.</u> Sometimes this is just necessary for many reasons, but it's definitely necessary if you are struggling with jealousy and envy! Take a social media break, and while you are on that break, be sure to keep a gratitude journal of all the amazing things that God is doing in your life!

Nikeya Young

Nice Women Finish First

So, you made it all the way to the end of this book! That means you are serious about God and the things of God, and you are ready to go out into the world and represent for the Kingdom! But perhaps in the back of your mind you hear the voice of your critics: "Boring!" they say. But I assure you; the very LAST word that can be used to describe a Virtue Chic Diva is "boring"! Think about it. Is anything about God "boring"? NO WAY! God is FULL of surprises, and so are His daughters!

Yes, it might seem like the women you see on television, in magazines, or films, who are not "virtuous women" have it going on. And to a certain extent, they do, but at what cost? They have only scratched the surface of what God intended for them to have. By seeking first the Kingdom of God and His Righteousness (God's way of doing and being right), all sorts of AMAZING things shall be added unto you (Matthew 6:33)! One thing I can say for Virtue Chics is that they STAND OUT! Men find them intriguing because:

1. They're covered up, so there's plenty left to the imagination.

2. Because they are not trying so hard to grab a man's attention, men are more interested to get to know them.

On the relationship end, VC's often have to be willing to be single a little while longer than most women. Why? We have higher standards! But, as I mentioned in my relationship testimony earlier in this book, the man that God has for you will not be put off by your standards. In fact, he will be attracted to them! A Virtue Chic Diva knows that it is better to be single and walking fully in her purpose than allowing herself to be test driven by men who have nothing to do with her God-given purpose! She has no time for distractions. She does not fear being alone, so she does not grow weary in well-doing and start to act out of character just because God didn't bring her the perfect man by her thirtieth birthday. Some of the most powerful people in the Bible were singles, like Jesus, Elijah, Elisha, Mary Magdalene, and the Apostle Paul, to name a few!

I am hoping that you are walking a little bit taller and holding your head a little higher after reading this book. By continuing to uphold the standard of righteousness in a world that wants to cut God completely out, you are serving as a beacon of light in the darkness. Do not let anything, or anyone dim your light

ACKNOWLEDGMENTS

I would like to say a very special thank you to Tiheasha Beasley and the entire November Media Publishing team for making my dream of becoming a published author a reality! You all are AMAZING and it has been a joy to work with you! To my spiritual leaders, Pastors Jerry and Chris McQuay: You two are two of the most humble, generous, kindest, ANOINTED leaders I've ever met! Thank you for embracing my family! We are proud members of Christian Life Center -Tinley Park Campus and we have grown tremendously! To Debbie and Julius Adebayo of Singles Pleasing the Lord (SPL), thank you SO MUCH for years of friendship, leadership, and accountability! It is a blessing to know you both, and we are honored to be a part of the SPL family! To my Marriage/Life Coaches Mama Love and Tony McPherson- you two are AWESOME! Thank you SO much for your prayers, words of wisdom and accountability over the years! Pastors Bill and Joyce

Gardner (rest in Heaven Pastor Bill) of Tulsa, Oklahoma; Bishop James C. Austin and First Lady Vernesta T. Austin of St. Luke Church of God in Christ in Chicago, Illinois; and Dr. Bill and Veronica Winston of Living Word Christian Center in Forest Park, Illinois; thank you all for the seeds of faith that you've planted and watered in me over the years!

To my dear friend Niki Winston, thanks SO much for writing such a beautiful Foreword! I love you and David so much! Thank you both for your love and support over the years! To my Big Sister Shaun Butler and my handsome nephews (Shauntarion and Shauntrevion Butler) I love you! Much love to my in-laws as well! Marionette and Rodney Young Sr., you have raised an AWESOME son! My life has been changed immensely. Thank you! To my "Fairy God-mothers": My beautiful Aunties - Sondra Terry (rest in Heaven), Helen Ray, Thelma Strong, Jennifer Smith, and Debbie Fisher, my beloved Stepmother/friend Linda Cox (Rest in Heaven), Mama Mosetta Ann Smith, and last but CERTAINLY not least- Deborah Thomas. Each of you ladies played an integral part in getting me from that "rocky age 14" stage after I'd just lost my mother to the strong, God-Fearing, VICTORIOUS woman I am today! From the bottom of my heart, THANK YOU! I have FAR too many friends and family members to name; but just know that I am VERY grateful for all of the love and support that I have received! Everyone always talks about having "haters". I have a few of those too (even JESUS had them)! However, the amount of people who genuinely love me, wish me well, encourage me in person and on social media, and who babysit my son so I can still go on auditions and dates with my husband (shout out to Tony and Ruby Powell and family, Tenia Hoskins and family, Bianca Medina, Amanda Edwards, Rachel and Jon Jones and Mom Thomas) I say thank you! Those who acknowledge/appreciate my gifts and invite me to share them with their churches/radio and television audiences are FAR greater than the small handful of people who are committed to not liking me no matter what I do! Believe it or not, I am grateful for those people too! Any time you make a BOLD stance for

God/Christian Living, you can expect attacks from the enemy! Just know that adversity is to Nikeya Young as spinach is to Popeye the Sailor Man!

And last, but not least…YOU! Thank you so much for investing your time and money into the Virtue Chic Brand! I pray that you were blessed and encouraged to walk boldly in your faith (and look FIERCE doing it), and live victoriously! Be sure to subscribe to my e-mail list at www.virtuechic.net to receive the latest blogs, events, and more!

MEET THE AUTHOR

Nikeya Young is a loving wife, mother, entertainer (Actress/member of SAG-AFTRA), Model, Christian Singer/Songwriter, Motivational Speaker, and all around "Renaissance Woman"! Nikeya graduated from DePaul University with a Bachelor of Arts Degree in Psychology. She earned her Master of Arts Degree in Special Education from Northeastern Illinois University and served as a Special Education Teacher in Chicago Public Schools for 5 years. She then pursued a career in the entertainment industry and used her God-given gifts of teaching, writing, and singing to inspire others to live a victorious life! In 2013, Nikeya released her debut album, Victorious One. The album was Executive Produced by Nikeya and her husband, Rodney. Victorious One received great reviews and earned her a "Contemporary Female Artist of the Year" nomination alongside Motown recording artist, Anita Wilson, and several others in the 2014 Chicago Gospel Music Awards.

Nikeya's national television appearances include multiple modeling appearances on The Steve Harvey Show, NBC's Chicago Fire, and TV One's Find Our Missing, alongside several commercials. As a fashion blogger, Nikeya has been featured in several media outlets such as The Chicago Tribune, PLUS Model Magazine, SKORCH Magazine, Global Grind, Examiner.com, and USA Today. Nikeya resides in the Chicagoland area with her husband, Rodney Young Jr., and their son, Rodney Price Young, III (R3).

In 2015, Nikeya combined her faith in God with her love for fashion and launched "Virtue Chic"- a brand and movement for every woman who has ever felt like they were the ONLY one who feels that modesty does NOT have to equal "frumpy"! You are NOT ALONE!

YOU CAN CONNECT WITH NIKEYA YOUNG

Visiting her website at www.nikeyayoung.com and following her on social media at:

Facebook.com/OfficialNikeyaYoung
Instagram: @nikeyayoung
Twitter: @nikeyayoung
Periscope: @nikeyayoung

For Booking, send an e-mail to
Booking@nikeyayoung.com

To join the "Virtue Chic" movement, visit www.virtuechic.net , and follow us on social media at:

Facebook.com/VirtueChic
Instagram: @virtuechic
Twitter: @virtuechic
Email: virtuechic@gmail.com

www.ingramcontent.com/pod-product-compliance
Lightning Source LLC
Chambersburg PA
CBHW070628300426
44113CB00010B/1701